D0821221

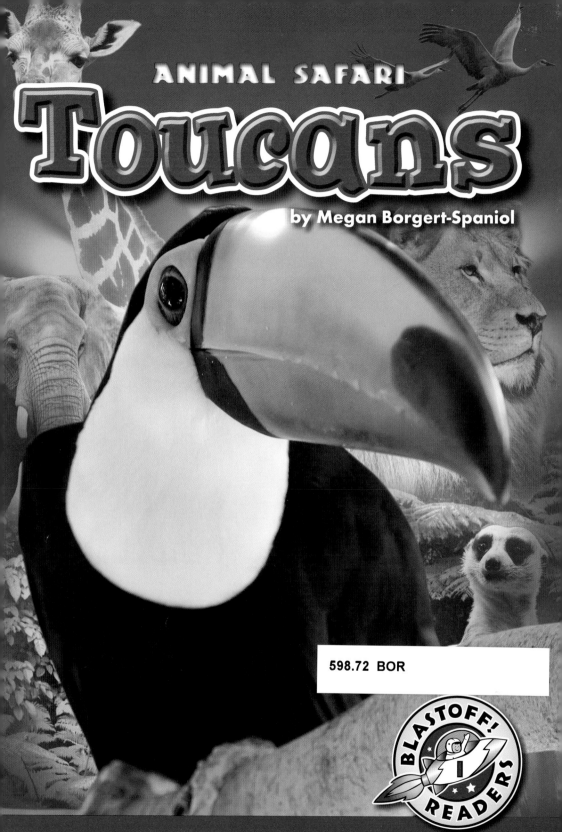

ANIMAL SAFARI

Toucans

by Megan Borgert-Spaniol

BLASTOFF! READERS

BELLWETHER MEDIA · MINNEAPOLIS, MN

Note to Librarians, Teachers, and Parents:

Blastoff! Readers are carefully developed by literacy experts and combine standards-based content with developmentally appropriate text.

Level 1 provides the most support through repetition of high-frequency words, light text, predictable sentence patterns, and strong visual support.

Level 2 offers early readers a bit more challenge through varied simple sentences, increased text load, and less repetition of high-frequency words.

Level 3 advances early-fluent readers toward fluency through increased text and concept load, less reliance on visuals, longer sentences, and more literary language.

Level 4 builds reading stamina by providing more text per page, increased use of punctuation, greater variation in sentence patterns, and increasingly challenging vocabulary.

Level 5 encourages children to move from "learning to read" to "reading to learn" by providing even more text, varied writing styles, and less familiar topics.

Whichever book is right for your reader, Blastoff! Readers are the perfect books to build confidence and encourage a love of reading that will last a lifetime!

This edition first published in 2014 by Bellwether Media, Inc.

No part of this publication may be reproduced in whole or in part without written permission of the publisher. For information regarding permission, write to Bellwether Media, Inc., Attention: Permissions Department, 5357 Penn Avenue South, Minneapolis, MN 55419.

Library of Congress Cataloging-in-Publication Data

Borgert-Spaniol, Megan, 1989- author.
 Toucans / by Megan Borgert-Spaniol.
  pages cm. – (Blastoff! Readers. Animal Safari)
 Summary: "Developed by literacy experts for students in kindergarten through grade three, this book introduces toucans to young readers through leveled text and related photos"– Provided by publisher.
 Audience: 5 to 8.
 Audience: K to grade 3.
 Includes bibliographical references and index.
  ISBN 978-1-62617-065-0 (hardcover : alk. paper)
 1. Toucans–Juvenile literature. I. Title. II. Series: Blastoff! readers. 1, Animal safari.
 QL696.P57B67 2014
 598.7'2–dc23
                                                              2013032317

Contents

What Are Toucans?

Toucans are birds with large **bills**.

They live in **rain forests**. Their bills match the colorful **canopy**.

Toucans do not fly well. Instead they hop from branch to branch.

Toucans have four strong toes on each foot. They help the birds **grasp** branches and climb trees.

Eating

Toucans use their bills to pick fruits from trees. They also eat **insects**, frogs, and lizards.

Sometimes toucans eat bird eggs. They grab the eggs from nests inside tree holes.

Flocks

Toucans travel in **flocks**. They call to one another with barks and croaks.

Sometimes they toss fruits to one another. They also **play-fight**.

Toucans often **roost** in groups. They rest their bills on their backs. Sleep tight, toucan!

Glossary

bills—the hard outer parts of the mouths of birds

canopy—a covering formed by the tops of trees; toucans live in the rain forest canopy.

flocks—groups of toucans that travel, eat, and roost together

grasp—to grab and hold tightly

insects—small animals with six legs and hard outer bodies; insect bodies are divided into three parts.

play-fight—to fight in a playful way

rain forests—warm, wet forests that get a lot of rain

roost—to rest or sleep

To Learn More

AT THE LIBRARY

Guidone, Julie. *Toucans and Other Birds*.
New York, N.Y.: Gareth Stevens Publishing,
2009.

Mayfield, Sue. *I Can, You Can, Toucan!*
New York, N.Y.: Crabtree Pub. Co., 2006.

Suen, Anastasia. *Toco Toucan: Bright Enough
to Disappear*. New York, N.Y.: Bearport,
2010.

ON THE WEB
Learning more about
toucans is as easy as 1, 2, 3.

1. Go to www.factsurfer.com.

2. Enter "toucans" into the search box.

3. Click the "Surf" button and you will see a
   list of related Web sites.

With factsurfer.com, finding more information
is just a click away.

Index

The images in this book are reproduced through the courtesy of: Geanina Bechea, front cover; Grafissimo, p. 5; Klein-Hubert/ Kimball Stock, p. 7; tbkmedia.de/ Alamy, p. 9; Eduardo Rivero, p. 11; Joe Austin Photography/ Alamy, p. 13; Dr. Morley Read, p. 13 (bottom left); Dirk Ercken, p. 13 (bottom middle); Steve Bower, p. 13 (bottom right); Biosphoto/ SuperStock, p. 15; Chin Kit Sen, p. 17; ariadna de raadt, p. 19; Alexey Danilchenko Photography, p. 21.